DON'T
MESS WITH A
WOMEN WHO
KNOWS HOW TO
STAGE A CRIME
SCENE

IT'S TIME
FOR WINE
AND TRUE
CRIME

SHHH I'M
LISTENING
TO TRUE
CRIME
PODCAST

INTROVERTED
BUT WILLING
TO TALK ANY
EAR OFF
ABOUT SERIAL
KILLERS

EAT SLEEP
SERIAL KILLER
DOCUMENTARI
ES REPEAT

IT'S A
GOOD TIME
FOR TRUE
CRIME

COFEE
AND
CRIME
SHOWS

SOUNDS
SUSPISH

I RUN ON
COFFE AND
MURDER
SHOWS

I KNOW MORE
NAMES OF SERIAL
KILLER THAN THE
POEPLE I WORK
WITH

I HAVE WATCHED SO
MANY TRUE CRIMES
SHOWS THAT I AM
READY TO EITHER
COMMIT OR SOLVE A
MURDER

ROSES ARE RED
VIOLETS ARE BLUE
I HAVE WATCHED
SO MANY CRIME
SHOWS THEY
NEVER FIND YOU

STRESSED
BLESSED &
TRUE CRIME
OBSESSED

YOU
INSPIRE
MY INNER
SERIAL
KILLER

DO YOU ASSUME
ALL TRASH BAGS
ON THE SIDE OF
THE ROAD ARE
BODY PARTS OR
ARE YOU
NORMAL?

FUELED BY
WINE AND
TRUE
CRIME

JUST A
NORMAL GIRL
WHO LOVES
MURDER
PODCASTS

SORRY I CAN'T
I'M WATCHING
SERIAL KILLER
DOCUMENTARIES

TRUE CRIME
IS JUST LIKE
A FAVORITE
WINE

I AM
BASICALLY
A
DETECTIVE

Made in the USA
Columbia, SC
23 December 2022

74912956R00024